Dedicated to Pastor Rick Zweck
who so generously shared his journey.

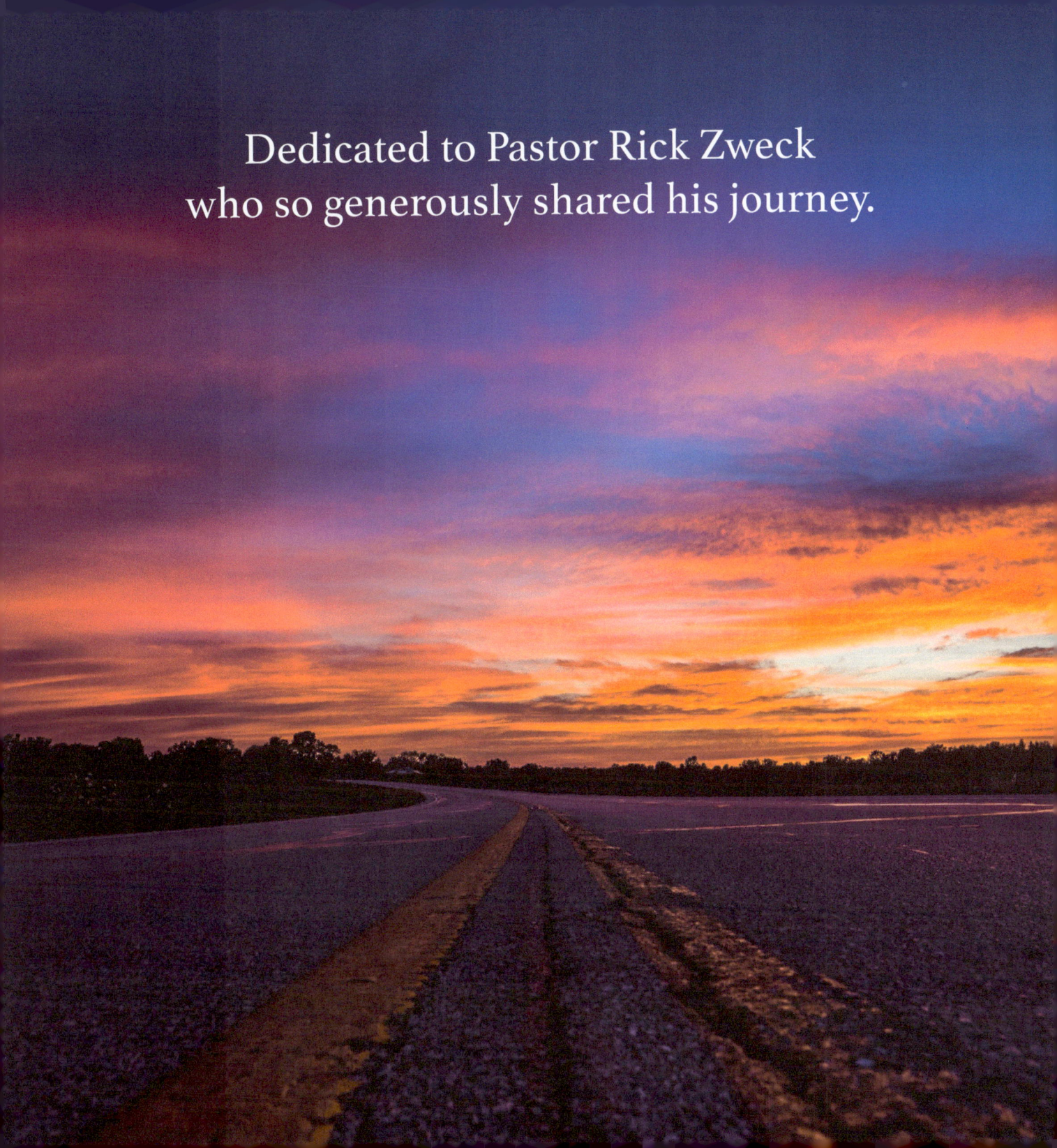

Ways To Use This Book

- Remember good places the pictures call to mind

- Wonder what's around the corner or over the horizon

- Find the common thing in every picture

- Sit together quietly, muse, discuss

- Explore the seven reflections

- Share a reading

- Pray one of the prayers

- Read a page with someone

- Journey together by reading a page each day

- Use it thoughtfully, with compassion, to show love.

Seven Reflections For The Journey

Steps of Christ on the road to resurrection...

I. Accepting The Path

When we realise that we may be on the journey home
we each react differently. As we travel we may feel angry,
afraid, cheated, guilty, numb, scared, or even relieved.

What have you felt lately?

It is healthy to share your feelings with someone you trust.

There is a time to fight and a time for acceptance...
But acceptance gives us power to do new things.

Jesus knew that the hour had come to leave
this world and return to the Father... - John 13:1b

There is a time for everything,
And a season for every activity under heaven:
A time to be born, and a time to die... - Ecclesiastes 3:1,2

2. Welcoming A Fellow Traveller

As we begin the journey home we may feel terribly alone.
We may even turn away others who try to share it with us.
But we need to welcome the fellow traveller.

Even if you feel that no one can join you on this road, Christ will.
You may not notice at first as He quietly walks beside you.
He will stay with you all the way, where others cannot go.

The Fellow Traveller is with you on this road already.
Notice him. Welcome him!

While they were talking and discussing together, Jesus himself drew near and went with them. But they did not recognise him.
- Luke 24:15-16

Jesus said, "I am with you always, even to the end of the age."
- Matthew 28:20

3. Lightening The Load

As we travel we need to hold on less tightly to some things.

There are some things we may need to grieve and let go of: possessions, plans, desires, or ambitions.

Letting go means less to worry about!

Ask for grace to let go of some things that weigh you down.

Unless a grain of wheat is planted in the soil and dies, it remains alone. But its death will produce a plentiful harvest of new life. Those who selfishly love their life in this world will lose it. Those who let go of their life in this world will keep it for eternity.
- John 12:24-26

4. Choosing Love

Sometimes we are tempted to fall into despair or self-pity. Christ was too. But he used his time to prepare those he loved.

Christ is with you and understands better than any what you're facing. Invite his Spirit to help you to love, to affirm, to encourage, and to leave people with peace.

In Christ, Love has chosen you;
Now you can choose love!

Having loved his own who were in the world, he loved them to the end... So he got up from the meal and wrapped a towel around his waist. He poured water into a basin and began to wash his disciples' feet, drying them with the towel that was wrapped around him... Jesus said, "Now I give you a new command: Love each other just as I have loved you."
- John 13:1-5,34

5. Forgiving

Although it may feel like a curse, actually knowing that you are on the road home is a gift of space that many do not receive. You may feel that time has been taken from you, but you now have a chance to do what matters most. The best thing to do is forgiveness – letting go!

Firstly, you may need forgiveness... Nothing is so bad that it cannot be shared with someone. Tell someone safe what burdens you. Speak to a caring friend, counsellor, or pastor and ask them to assure you that God forgives you. It will bring peace.

Secondly, this is a time to forgive... Choose to let go of the hurt others have inflicted on you. Whether or not they receive your forgiveness you can still choose to let go. Christ has forgiven you everything, and is with you to help you forgive.

There they crucified him, and the criminals, one on his right and one on his left. And Jesus said, "Father, forgive them, for they know not what they do."
- Luke 23:33-34

6. Handing Over

A time will come to let go of this life and all you hold on to.
When it comes, relax and trust.

You will receive far more than you hand over.
Commit yourself to God and let go.

Jesus, calling out with a loud voice, said,
"Father, into your hands I commit my spirit!"
And having said this he breathed his last.   - Luke 23:46

"In your hands I place my body and soul and all that is mine."
 - Martin Luther's Evening Prayer

7. Arriving Home

Think of a place where you were truly at peace.
Cherish this memory, hold it in your mind...

This is a small glimpse of the true Home called 'heaven'.
Heaven is not an entirely foreign destination, but is the real
home we yearn for. You may have had glimpses already!

As you come to God in humility you are welcome.
You have nothing to fear. The journey leads Home.

*Do not let your hearts be troubled. Trust in God, and trust also
in me. There is more than enough room in my Father's home.
If this were not so, would I have told you that I am going to
prepare a place for you? When everything is ready, I will
come and get you, so that you will be with me where I am.
And you know the way to where I am going... I am the way..."*
- John 14:1-4,6

Prayers & Readings

Encouragement for the road...

The Camino Call

Set out!
You were born for the road.

Set out!
You have a meeting to keep.
Where? With whom?
You'll see.

Set out!
Your steps will be your words,
The road your song,
The weariness your prayers,
And at the end silence will
speak.

Set out!
You were born for the road,
The Pilgrim's road.

Set out!
Your head does not know
Where your feet will lead your heart,
But the Guide will be with you,
Walking before you.

Set out!
Someone is coming to meet you
Seeking you
In the shrine at the road's end,
In the depths of your heart.
He is your peace.
He is your joy.

Go!
God walks with you.

- By Pastor Rick Zweck (1953 - 2016)

** Camino is Spanish for 'road' or 'journey' and is the title
of a famous pilgrimage which Rick cherished so much.*

I Will Not Fear

I do not see the road ahead.
I cannot know for certain where it will end.
But I know that you will lead me the right way
though I may know nothing about it.
Therefore, will I trust you always
though I may seem to be lost in the shadow of death.
I will not fear,
for you are ever with me,
and you never leave me
to face my perils alone.

- Adapted from words by Thomas Merton (1915 - 1968)

The Lord Is My Shepherd

The Lord is my Shepherd,
I shall not want.
He makes me lie down in green pastures,
He leads me beside quiet waters,
He restores my soul.
He guides me in paths of righteousness for his name's sake.

Even though I walk through the valley of the shadow of death,
I will fear no evil, for you are with me,
Your rod and your staff, they comfort me.
You prepare a table before me in the presence of my enemies.
You anoint my head with oil; my cup overflows.

Surely goodness and love will follow me all the days of my life,
and I will live in the house of the Lord forever.

- Psalm 23

Awakening Prayer

Awaken us to delight in your praises,
For You made us for Yourself
And our hearts are restless,
Until they rest in you.

- Augustine of Hippo (354 - 430)

For we know that when this earthly tent we live in is taken down (that is, when we die and leave this earthly body), we will have a house in heaven, an eternal body made for us by God himself and not by human hands.

- 2 Corinthians 5:1-2

Prayer For Peace

God grant me the serenity
To accept the things I cannot change,
The courage to change the things I can,
And the wisdom to know the difference.
Living one day at a time,
Enjoying one moment at a time,
Accepting hardship as a pathway to peace,
Taking, as you did, this world as it is,
Not as I want it,
Trusting that you will make all things right,
That I may be content in this life,
And joyful with you forever in the next.

- Reinhold Niebuhr (1892 - 1971)

Seeking Rest

I heard the voice of Jesus say
"Come unto me and rest,
Lay down your weary head lay down
Your head upon my chest."
I came to Jesus as I was,
Weary and worn and sad.
I found in him a resting place
and He has made me glad.

- Horatius Bonar (1808-1889)

Then Jesus said, "Come to me, all of you who are weary and carry heavy burdens, and I will give you rest.   Take my yoke upon you. Let me teach you, because I am humble and gentle of heart, and you will find rest for your soul." - Matthew 11:28-29

A Prayer Of Trust

O God, early in the morning I cry to you,
Help me to pray and to focus on you.
I cannot do this alone;
In me is darkness, but with you there is light.
I am lonely, but you do not leave me.
I am feeble, but with you is strength.
I am restless, but with you there is peace.
I do not understand your ways,
But you know the way for me.
Lord, whatever this day may bring,
Your name be praised.

- Dietrich Bonhoeffer (1906 - 1945)

For Things Still Undone

Complete One,
You know that sometimes I fret
About what is left unfinished.

Catch me when I fall backwards toward regret.
Call my heart to this precious moment.
Grace this very breath.

Nothing I ever did was fully perfect,
But Your grace makes all whole.

So I trust that in You
The incomplete is and will be
Complete.

- Matt Thiele

I Arise Today

I arise today
Through the strength of heaven,
Light of the sun, splendour of fire,
Speed of lightning, Swiftness of the wind,
Depth of the sea, Stability of the earth,
Firmness of the Rock.

Christ with me, Christ before me, Christ behind me,
Christ in me, Christ beneath me, Christ above me,
Christ on my right, Christ on my left,
Christ when I lie down, Christ when I sit down,
Christ in the heart of everyone who thinks of me,
Christ in the mouth of everyone who speaks of me,
Christ in the eye that sees me,
Christ in the ear that hears me.

I arise today
Through the mighty strength
Of the Lord of creation.

- St Patrick (385 - 461)

I Lift My Eyes To The Hills

I lift up my eyes to the hills.
Where does my help come from?
My help comes from the Lord who made heaven and earth!

God will not let your foot be moved, God will not sleep.
See, the one who guards you will neither slumber nor sleep.
The Lord is your keeper;
The Lord is is the shade by your side.
The sun shall not strike you by day, nor the moon by night.

The Lord will keep you from all evil and will keep your life.
The Lord will keep your going out and your coming in
From this time forth and forevermore.

- Psalm 121

I Am Still With You

I praise you
because I am fearfully and wonderfully made.
Your works are wonderful; I know that full well.
My body was not hidden from you
when I was made in the secret place,
when I was woven together in the depths of the womb.
Your eyes saw my unformed body,
all the days ordained for me were written in your book
before one of them came to be.
How precious to me are your thoughts, God.
How vast is the sum of them!
They outnumber the grains of sand.
When I awake, I am still with you.

- Psalm 139:14-18

A Prayer In Pain

O God,
I am struck down to my lowest.
Pain consumes my world.
The more I think of it the worse it is.
It beggars my brain, it fogs my senses,
It reduces my world to a searing endless struggle.

I call out to you, Jesus,
The crucified, betrayed, buried, descended One,
You bore this pain, You lived this pain, You beat this pain.
And if you, God, can be on that 'God-forsaken' cross,
Then you can be with me here.

Come Holy Spirit and let me use this time to give,
So that even in this moment of helplessness,
I may share Your love with the World.

Thank you Jesus, that you share this pain.

- Matt Thiele

The Prayer Of St. Francis

Lord, make me an instrument of your peace.
Where there is hatred, let me sow love,
Where there is injury, pardon,
Where there is doubt, faith,
Where there is despair, hope,
Where there is darkness, light,
Where there is sadness, joy.

O Master, grant that I may not so much seek
To be consoled as to console,
To be understood as to understand,
To be loved as to love.
For it is in giving that we receive,
It is in pardoning that we are pardoned;
And it is in dying that we are born to Eternal Life.

- Saint Francis Of Assisi (1181 - 1226)

Abide With Me

Abide with me, fast falls the eventide.
The darkness deepens, Lord with me abide.
When other helpers fail and comforts flee,
Help of the helpless, O abide with me.

Hold thou thy cross before my closing eyes.
Shine through the gloom, and point me to the skies.
Heaven's morning breaks, and earth's vain shadows flee,
In life, in death, O Lord, abide with me.

- Henry Francis Lyte (1793 – 1847)

The Ground Breaking

It is the third day
since the ground won.

It is the third day
since the grave claimed
His beaten flesh.

It is the third day.

Shock begins to lapse
Into the long silence of loss.
This is what comes after 'it is finished.'

But...

The ground begins to break.

The Beast ate something
that does not agree with it!

Death's belly throbs for three days.
The bowels of the Deep groan.
An abyss with indigestion;
Hell swelling with sick stomach.
It cannot digest Him,
It cannot possess Him.

Hell fails,
Death pales,
Life prevails,
The ground abounds,
As earth gives birth,
For this tomb is a womb.
Yes, this tomb is a womb!

A voice of triumph,
A seismic shout of victory,
An earthquake of joy!
Every grain of dust dancing,
Tallest trees trembling,
Great mountains rattling,
Sun and stars singing,
As the Tidal Wave of Life breaks the ground.

The heavenly host watch in awe,
As the angel reverently rolls away the stone;
Not so Christ can break out,
But so all can see in.

Now all can see that
The ground has been broken!

- Matt Thiele (Easter 2017)

The Lord Is My Light

The Lord is my light and my salvation, whom shall I fear?

Hear my voice when I call, Lord.
Be merciful to me and answer me.
My heart says, "Seek God's face"
Your face I will seek!

Do not reject me or forsake me, God my Saviour.
Though my father and mother forsake me,
The Lord will receive me.

Teach me your way, Lord, lead me in a straight path...

I remain confident of this:
I will see the goodness of the Lord
In the land of the living.

Wait for the Lord.
Be strong and take heart
And wait for the Lord!

- Psalm 27 (selected verses)

Habakkuk's Prayer Of Hope

Though the fig tree does not bud
and there are no grapes on the vines,
though the olive crop fails
and the fields produce no food,
though there are no sheep in the pen
and no cattle in the stalls.

Yet I will rejoice in the Lord,
I will be joyful in God my Saviour.
The Sovereign Lord is my strength;
God makes my feet like the feet of a deer,
God enables me to walk the heights!

- Habakkuk 3:17–19

Closer Than Breathing

Lord, you are closer to me
than my own breathing,
nearer than my hands and feet.

– St Teresa of Avila (1515-1582)

You surround me,
Behind and before,
Your hand is upon me.
Where can I go from your Spirit?
Where can I flee from your presence?
If I go up to the heavens, you are there;
If I make my bed in the depths, you are there.
If I rise on the wings of the dawn,
If I settle on the far side of the sea,
Even there your hand will guide me,
Your right hand will hold me fast.
If I say, "Surely the darkness will hide me
And the light become night around me,"
Even the darkness will not be dark to you;
The night will shine like the day,
For darkness is as light to you.
- Psalm 139:5-12

Flying And Catching

One day, I was sitting with Rodleigh, the leader of the troupe, in his caravan, talking about flying. He said, "As a flyer, I must have complete trust in my catcher. The public might think that I am the greatest star of the trapeze, but the real star is Joe, my catcher. He has to be there for me with split-second precision and grab me out of the air as I come to him in the long jump."
"How does it work?" I asked. "The secret," Rodleigh said, "is that the flyer does nothing and the catcher does everything: when I fly to Joe, I have simply to stretch out my arms and hands and wait for him to catch me and pull me safely over the apron behind the catchbar." "You do nothing!" I said, surprised. "Nothing," Rodleigh repeated. "A flyer must fly, and a catcher must catch, and the flyer must trust, with outstretched arms, that his catcher will be there for him." When Rodleigh said this with so much conviction, the words of Jesus flashed through my mind: "Father into your hands I commend my Spirit." Dying is trusting in the catcher. To care for the dying is to say, "Don't be afraid. Remember that you are the beloved child of God. He will be there when you make your long jump. Don't try to grab him; he will grab you. Just stretch out your arms and hands and trust, trust, trust."

- Henri J. M. Nouwen (1932-1996)
 From *Our Greatest Gift: A Meditation On Dying And Caring.*

A Prayer To The Holy Spirit

Holy Spirit,
Comforting fire, Life of all creation.
Anointing the sick, cleansing body and soul,
Fill this body!

Holy Spirit,
Sacred breath, Fire of love,
Sweetest taste, Beautiful aroma,
Fill this heart!

Holy Spirit,
Filling the world, from the heights to the deep,
Raining from clouds, filling rivers and sea,
Fill this mind!

Holy Spirit,
Forgiving and giving, uniting strangers, reconciling enemies,
Seeking the lost, and enfolding us together,
Fill these gathered here!

Holy Spirit,
Bringing light into dark places, igniting praise,
Greatest gift, our Hope and Encourager,
Holy Spirit of Christ,
I praise you! Amen.

– Adapted from a prayer of Hildegard of Bingen (1098-1179)

The Lord's Prayer

Our Father in heaven,
Hallowed be your name,
Your kingdom come,
Your will be done on earth as in heaven.
Give us today our daily bread.
Forgive us our sins
as we forgive those who sin against us.
Lead us not into temptation,
but deliver us from evil.
For the kingdom, the power,
and the glory are yours
now and forever.
Amen.

www.ingramcontent.com/pod-product-compliance
Lightning Source LLC
Chambersburg PA
CBHW042011090426
42811CB00015B/1612